A NOTE TO PARENTS

When your children are ready to "step into reading," giving them the right books is as crucial as giving them the right food to eat. **Step into Reading Books** present exciting stories and information reinforced with lively, colorful illustrations that make learning to read fun, satisfying, and worthwhile. They are priced so that acquiring an entire library of them is affordable. And they are beginning readers with a difference—they're written on five levels.

Early Step into Reading Books are designed for brand-new readers, with large type and only one or two lines of very simple text per page. **Step 1 Books** feature the same easy-to-read type as the Early Step into Reading Books, but with more words per page. **Step 2 Books** are both longer and slightly more difficult, while **Step 3 Books** introduce readers to paragraphs and fully developed plot lines. **Step 4 Books** offer exciting nonfiction for the increasingly independent reader.

The grade levels assigned to the five steps—preschool through kindergarten for the Early Books, preschool through grade 1 for Step 1, grades 1 through 3 for Step 2, grades 2 through 3 for Step 3, and grades 2 through 4 for Step 4—are intended only as guides. Some children move through all five steps very rapidly; others climb the steps over a period of several years. Either way, these books will help your child "step into reading" in style!

Text copyright © 2000 by Joyce Milton. Illustrations copyright © 2000 by Richard Courtney.
All rights reserved under International and Pan-American Copyright Conventions.
Published in the United States by Random House, Inc., New York, and simultaneously
in Canada by Random House of Canada Limited, Toronto.

www.randomhouse.com/kids

Library of Congress Cataloging-in-Publication Data
Milton, Joyce.
Heavy-duty trucks / by Joyce Milton ; illustrated by Richard Courtney.
p. cm. — (Step into reading. A step 2 book)
SUMMARY: Describes different kinds of trucks, including tractor-trailers, auto haulers, garbage trucks,
bulldozers, dump trucks, and cranes. ISBN 0-679-88130-1 (pbk.) — ISBN 0-679-98130-6 (lib. bdg.)
1. Trucks—Juvenile literature. [1. Trucks.] I. Courtney, Richard, ill. II. Title. III. Series.
TL230.15.M55 2000 629.224—dc21   99-14349

Printed in the United States of America February 2000 10 9 8 7 6 5 4 3 2 1

Step into Reading®

HEAVY-DUTY TRUCKS

By Joyce Milton
Illustrated by Richard Courtney

A Step 2 Book

Random House New York

On a busy highway,
huge trucks
go whizzing by.
What would it be like
to drive a really big truck?

Truckers shift gears a lot.
Big trucks have ten gears—
or more!

They talk to other drivers
on their CB radios.

Sometimes truckers
even sleep in their trucks.
Many big trucks have a bed
behind the driver's seat.
Truckers call this bed
the <u>sleeping</u> <u>box</u>.

There are two kinds
of trucks on the road.
Some trucks are all in one piece.
They are called <u>straight</u> <u>trucks</u>.

But the biggest trucks
have two parts.
They are called
tractor-trailers.
The driver sits
in the tractor, or cab.
Cargo goes in back,
in the trailer.

Some trailers have
eight wheels in back
and none at all in front.
They are called <u>semi-trailers</u>,
or <u>semis</u>, for short.
The front of the semi
rests on metal legs.

The truckdriver

hooks the semi to his cab.

Then he raises the legs.

Now he is ready

to hit the road.

Tractor-trailers can haul almost anything.

There is room
inside this moving van
for a whole houseful
of furniture.

<u>Open-bed</u> trailers

are trailers with open sides.

They carry the heaviest loads.

These logs are on their way

to the sawmill.

Eight brand-new cars
can ride piggyback
on an <u>auto</u> <u>hauler</u>.

Some trailers are
huge refrigerators on wheels.
Truckers call them <u>reefers</u>.
Reefers carry meat,
frozen foods,
and even candy bars.

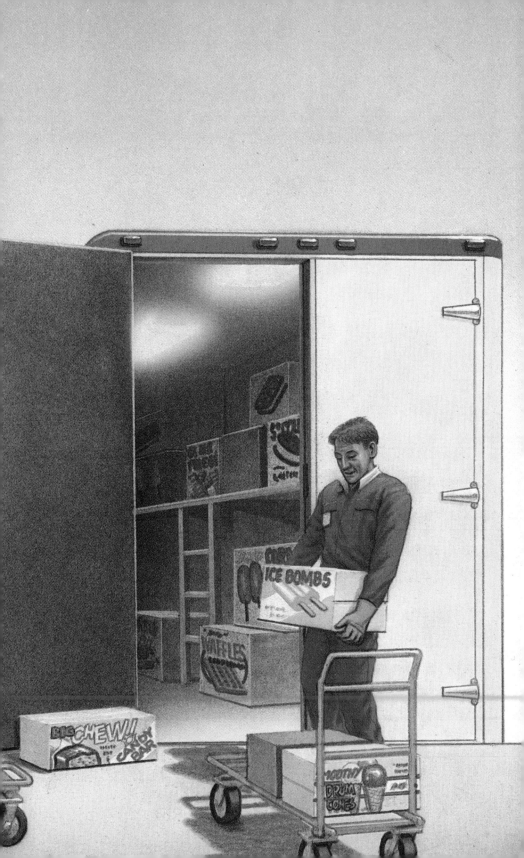

Other trucks carry live animals—
horses, cattle, chickens,
and sometimes beehives.

Once, a truck hauling beehives

was in an accident.

The driver was all right.

But thousands of bees escaped.

They were shook up and angry.

Beekeepers spent days

rounding them up.

A <u>tractor</u> is an important
truck for a farmer.
It pulls machines
that help work the fields.
One machine plants corn.

Another picks the corn
when it is ripe.

Inside the tractor's cab

there is a computer

that runs the planter.

There is a CD player, too.

The farmer can listen to music

while he picks the corn.

Cities need big trucks, too.
The <u>street</u> <u>sweeper</u> is like
a giant broom on wheels.

Garbage <u>trucks</u> carry away trash—
tons of it!

This truck is called

a <u>cherry picker.</u>

Is it used for picking cherries?

No!

This worker needs to fix

a broken power line.

She rides the cherry picker

up, up, up into the air.

Fire trucks race
to a burning building.
The <u>pumper</u> <u>truck</u>
pumps water from
a fire hydrant.

The <u>ladder</u> <u>truck</u>
carries a ladder
tall enough to reach
a fifth-story window.

One firefighter hears a scream.
He climbs up the ladder
and carries a child
down to safety.

There's a new building
going up in town.
Here's your chance
to see some special
heavy-duty trucks.

The <u>bulldozer</u>

is the first to go to work.

It pushes heavy rocks

and piles of dirt

out of the way.

Backhoes dig holes.
The scoop on the back end
of the backhoe
is called a bucket.
The bucket can hold
almost a ton of dirt.

This giant backhoe
is called a <u>trackhoe</u>.
That's because it has tracks
instead of wheels.
The tracks keep it
from sinking into the mud.

The trackhoe is digging
a deep hole.
The hole will become
the building's underground
parking garage.

Carrying away

tons of dirt

is a job for a monster

<u>dump</u> <u>truck.</u>

This one's wheels
are twelve feet high—
twice as tall as a grown man.
The driver has to use a ladder
to get to his seat.

<u>Cranes</u> are the weightlifters
of the truck family.
The crane's long arm
lifts steel beams
high into the air.
Driving a crane
can be dangerous.
One mistake, and the crane
can tip right over.

The tallest cranes
are called <u>tower</u> <u>cranes</u>.
This tower crane
is eight stories tall.

Cranes are not always used
to put up new buildings.
They also tear
old buildings down.
Workers use a <u>wrecker</u> <u>crane</u>
for this big job.

When the driver swings
the heavy metal ball,
watch out!
Bricks go flying everywhere.

The biggest trucks of all

are used for building roads.

This <u>pavement</u> <u>profiler</u>

is as wide as

a four-lane highway.

Its giant teeth

chew up the old pavement.

A <u>concrete</u> <u>mixer</u>
is like a giant blender.
The drum turns
to mix the concrete.
Then it pours it out
onto the roadbed.

Another extra-wide truck,
called a <u>spreader</u>,
spreads the wet concrete
across the road.

Soon the new highway

will be filled with cars.

And trucks, too—

lots of them.

Trucks keeping our
store shelves
filled with good things.
Trucks doing all kinds
of heavy-duty jobs.

The next time
you take a ride,
look out the window.
How many heavy-duty
trucks can you name?